Preface

Welcome to a comprehensive resource tailored specifically for students of the Foundation Course in English–II. **"IGNOU BCA Foundation Course in English 2 Previous Year Unsolved Papers FEG 02"** has been meticulously crafted to support learners in their academic journey by providing access to a collection of previous years' unsolved question papers.

As students navigate the intricacies of English language and literature, gaining familiarity with past examination patterns and question types becomes an essential part of effective preparation. This book is designed to help students strengthen their understanding of the subject while also developing the skills necessary to tackle examinations with confidence.

Each question paper has been presented in its original format to simulate a real exam environment. Practicing with these authentic papers enables students to manage their time effectively, understand the structure and style of questions, and sharpen their analytical and writing skills.

The primary goal of this book is to empower students to express their knowledge and ideas clearly and confidently. By actively engaging with the unsolved papers, students can identify key focus areas, evaluate their progress, and refine their preparation strategies.

We sincerely hope that this book becomes a valuable companion in your exam preparation journey and contributes meaningfully to your success in the Foundation Course in English–II.

INDEX

Table of Contents

BDP/BCA/BTS

Chapter 1: Term-End Examination, June- 2014

FEG-2: FOUNDATION COURSE IN ENGLISH-2

Time: 2 Hours

Maximum Marks: 50

Note: Answer all questions.

1. Write a composition in about 350 words on any one of the following: 20

(a) Joint family system: A blessing for modern society.

(b) The Changing face of cinema today.

(c) Qualities that make a leader.

(d) Great is the struggle and great is also the prize.

2. Write a paragraph in about 200 words on any one of the following: 10

(a) Reasons to protect and preserve historical monuments.

(b) The importance of personal grooming and hygiene.

(c) Girls' education and the family.

(d) Child labour - A curse for society.

3. (a) You are a newspaper reporter. Write a report on a half-marathon organised by a mobile network service provider. Give details of the number of people, young and old, who participated, sponsors who advertised their products, incentives given to participants, and other details related to arrangements by traffic police.

Or

(b) A new school has been set up in the village where your cousins live. They do not attend any school. Write a letter to your uncle, persuading him to admit his three children to the newly opened school, emphasizing the advantages of education in today's world. 10

4. Summarize the following passage in not more than 100 words and give it a suitable title:

Passage: **10**

There are a number of "wealths" other than the material wealth which relates to money and physical assets. But there is another important wealth which is not generally acknowledged and that is the inner wealth of our mind, our consciousness. This mind is like a wish-fulfilling jewel. If you know how to utilise this mind, it can produce the most beneficial effects. The best way to utilise and develop this mind is to absorb knowledge and the most important kind of knowledge is the one that makes us a kind person, a decent person, a person worthy of respect.

The qualities which make an individual kind, decent, and respectable are qualities such as patience, generosity, and kindness. The good news is that we do not have to adopt or create these qualities, since they are already potentially there in all of us. In this way, the wealth lies latent within each and every one of us.

So, all we need to do is give ourselves, every day, a bit of a reason to generate these qualities, bit by bit. If we do this, it will not make society perfect, but it will enable us to appreciate whatever circumstances we might face. As such, we have to be grateful for obstacles because without them we never learn. It is thanks to difficulties and challenges that we can come up with solutions, some of which will work and some not. But even if they don't work, it doesn't mean we should give up. It only means we should try again.

BDP / BCA / BTS

Chapter 2: Term-End Examination, December- 2014

FEG-2 : FOUNDATION COURSE IN ENGLISH-2

Time: 2 Hours

Maximum Marks: 50

Note: Attempt all questions.

1. Write a composition in about 350 words on any one of the following: 20

(a) Erosion in Human Values in Modern Times

(b) Ways of Reaching out to Disadvantaged People

(c) Our Dependence on Gadgets

(d) Disaster Management: The Need of the Hour

2. Write a paragraph in about 200 words on any one of the following topics: 10

(a) Preventing Road Mishaps

(b) The Importance of Cultivating a Hobby

(c) The World as a Global Society

(d) Role of the Media in creating Public Awareness

3. (a) A children's park in your colony has been encroached upon by a builder. As a result, children are not able to use the park. Write a letter to the Ward Officer, Municipal Corporation (of your city), bringing this to his/her notice and requesting him/her to help restore the park to its original shape and use.

OR

(b) You have joined an NGO named 'Clean and Green India' that is dedicated to bringing about awareness about hygiene and cleanliness. As part of the activities, you have gone on cleanliness drives, performed street plays, and made home visits carrying your message. Describe your experiences at 'Clean and Green India' to your friend. (10)

4. Summarize the following passage to not more than one-third of the original. Give it a suitable title: **10**

Passage:

Through his art, Mario Miranda, who passed away in Goa on December 11, 2011, taught us to laugh at our faults and shortcomings. He would capture the spirit of a man very well, using expressions and typical behaviour. He would draw cartoons about the lives of taxi drivers, bus drivers, secretaries working in offices, and families from different religions, and make us smile. He used to draw illustrations and cartoons of his teachers in school. He had no formal education in art when he started out as an illustrator in one of the leading newspapers in Mumbai. He could capture moments from daily life and freeze them in his art like no other.

Not just his cartoons and illustrations but his landscapes of Goa — cathedrals, crossroads, the people of Goa — and also of his travels to Israel and Greece were beautiful. He was a prolific artist; he would draw one cartoon, or maybe more, every day.

As a person, Mario was very generous; he never had money on his mind. He was simple and genuine; one could call him a son of the soil. He returned to Goa about 12 years ago, after he retired from the newspaper he used to work with. He lived in a very small apartment in Colaba in Mumbai, but his house in Goa was palatial. He loved his house and his hometown.

BDP / BCA / BTS

Chapter 3: Term-End Examination, June 2015

FEG-2 : FOUNDATION COURSE IN ENGLISH-2

Time: 2 hours

Maximum Marks: 50

Note: Attempt all questions.

1. Write a composition in about 350 words on any one of the following: 20

(a) Advantages of Distance Education

(b) The Rights of the Girl Child

(c) Waste Management in India

(d) Living Healthy is Living Happy

2. Write a paragraph in about 200 words on any one of the given topics: 10

(a) Overcoming Physical Challenges

(b) Monsoon in India

(c) Major Problems of India's Megacities

(d) Preservation of Cultural Values

3. (a) You are a Human Resource (HR) Manager in a textile factory. Recently there was unrest in the factory. The situation was brought under control by their new young leader. Write a letter to the editor of a national newspaper, citing the example of this union leader, making a case for responsible leadership.

OR

(b) Your cousin has failed in an interview for a job and is depressed. Write a letter to her suggesting possible options and advising her to meet a career counsellor. 10

4. Summarize the following passage to not more than one-third of the original length. Give it a suitable title 10

Passage:

An empty plastic bottle, a litre of water, and a few spoons of bleach — that's all that the students of IIT Powai needed to bring light to the homes of slum dwellers in Gowandi. Inspired by Isang Litrong Liwanag's campaign carried out successfully by the 'My Shelter Foundation' in the Philippines, students of the department of metallurgical engineering and material science decided to bring light to the dingy rooms of Mumbai slums.

Noticing the simplicity of the Solar Bottle Bulb, the group worked for over four months to bring the simple but ingenious idea to light. A Solar Bottle Bulb is a clear water bottle with tap water and a little bleach. This bottle is then embedded into the roofs of houses, with part of the bottle outside, and part inside. The water inside the bottle makes the light omni-directional, mimicking an electric light bulb. The bleach keeps the water clear for years. The group visited the slums and found that rooms were so close to each other that even the passage between them had close to no light even during the daytime. Inside the room, at least one tube or bulb was required all through the day, pushing their electricity bills to 400 — 600 each month.

The students constructed a few samples to show the residents how they worked. They could not just drill a hole in their roofs; they needed them to like the idea. To their delight, everyone liked the concept. The advantage of the Solar Bottle Bulb is that it has a very simple process using very simple things. The only drawback of the Solar Bottle Bulb is that it is functional only from sunrise till sunset. Even then, the electricity it saves during the day is reason enough for the slum dwellers to use it.

BDP / BCA / BTS

Chapter 4: Term-End Examination, December- 2015

FEG-2 : FOUNDATION COURSE IN ENGLISH-2

Time: 2 hours

Maximum Marks: 50

Note: Answer all questions.

1. Write a composition in about 350 words on any one of the following topics: 20

(a) A day in the life of a working woman

(b) The education system of India only produces clerks

(c) A long life — a curse or a boon?

(d) An unforgettable journey

2. Write a paragraph in about 200 words on any one of the following topics: 10

(a) Buying a mobile phone

(b) Life in a small town

(c) Changing fashions

(d) Joint family system

3. Write a report in about 200 words on the following: 10

(a) As part of a project on leisure activities of youth, you conducted a survey of five colonies in your neighbourhood. Write a short report about the survey highlighting:

- the information gathered,
- conclusions, and
- recommendations

OR

(b) A hospital has started a regular free health-check camp in your town for the economically weaker sections of society. As a reporter for a local newspaper, you visited the camp. Write a report highlighting what the hospital is doing.

4. Read the following passage, make notes, and give it a suitable title: 10

Passage:

If a learning difficulty has caused you humiliation, shame, defeat, or anxiety, as it often does while you are growing up, then it's likely that you tried to hide it away in some private compartment of your life and developed defensive strategies for dealing with it. Sally Smith, a well-known writer, says that there are many different 'masks' that people with learning problems wear to protect their self-esteem such as the mask of the 'clown', the mask of the 'victim' or the mask of 'invisibility'. It is said that these masks protect and defend them against the painful feelings connected with not feeling 'okay' as a learner.

Sometimes these masks actually are helpful in furthering a person's work-life or relationships. But at other times these masks get in the way of growth and need to be discarded. Many individuals with learning problems talk about the relief they felt once they began to speak openly about their difficulties. A student at a school for learning-disabled adults said, 'I feel like a leaden weight has been lifted off my shoulders by not having to pretend to be having a riotous time and not having to think up all those quips. I have energy now for my studies.

BDP / BCA / BTS

Chapter 5: Term-End Examination, June- 2016

FEG-2 : FOUNDATION COURSE IN ENGLISH-2

Time: 2 hours

Maximum Marks: 50

Note: Answer all questions.

1. Write a composition in about 350 words on any one of the following topics: 20

(a) The cultural diversity of India

(b) A visit to a historical place

(c) Educating the girl child

(d) A day in the life of a working woman

2. Write a paragraph in about 200 words on any one of the following topics: 10

(a) Buying a birthday present

(b) Indian festivals

(c) Life in a big city

(d) Cha

3. Write a report in about 200 words on the following: 10

(a) As part of a project on environment protection, you conducted a survey of five colonies in your neighbourhood to see what people are doing to save the environment. Write a short report about the survey highlighting:

• the information gathered,

• conclusions, and

• recommendations.

OR

(b) A non-government organisation has started a free school in your town. In six months' time, the project has received tremendous response from jhuggi clusters in the area. As a reporter for a local newspaper, you visited the school. Write a report for your newspaper highlighting what the school is doing to provide quality education.

4. Read the following passage, make notes, and give it a suitable title: 10

Passage:

The single-most important guideline to keep in mind when tackling learning problems is this: don't let your learning difficulties get in the way of being a successful human being. The problem with the term 'learning disabled' is that the learner might over-identify with it and begin to see herself as a handicapped individual. This can have a devastating effect upon one's self-worth. See yourself as an intact and whole human being before anything else. Then regard your learning difficulties simply as something that makes you an even richer and more unique human being.

Many successful individuals with learning problems have discovered that they can bypass their difficulties and find alternative ways of getting the job done. The famed inventor and industrialist Henry Ford had difficulty reading and remembering facts. He built a multi-million dollar empire by overcoming these disabilities in a different way. He surrounded himself with people who could answer any question he desired to ask concerning the business to which he was devoting most of his effort. As he himself said, 'Why should I clutter up my mind with general knowledge for the purpose of being able to answer questions, when I have men around me who can supply any knowledge I require?'

BDP / BCA / BTS

Chapter 6: Term-End Examination, December- 2016

FEG-2 : FOUNDATION COURSE IN ENGLISH-2

Time: 2 hours

Maximum Marks: 50

Note: Answer all questions.

1. Write a composition in about 350 words on any one of the following: 20

(a) Awareness of sexual abuse — a must in school education.

(b) The underprivileged child has every right to be educated.

(c) Pollution as a health hazard needs immediate attention.

(d) The newspaper is a welcome source of information.

2. Write a paragraph in about 200 words on any one of the following topics: 10

(a) Road Rage

(b) Technology can revolutionize education

(c) Happiness in families spending time together

(d) Time Management

3. Write a report on one of the following in about 200 words: 10

(a) You have been a witness to a fight between neighbours. As a result, one of the neighbours had to be hospitalised. Write a report for a local newspaper about the whole incident. Do report on the exact time of the incident, the likely causes, the casualties, and how such incidents can be avoided in the future.

OR

(b) Give reasons to support the statement: "Learning a second language extends one's vision and expands the mind. A second language teaches us different ways of labelling and organizing our experience." Your writing should explain, analyse, define, compare, and illustrate the statement given above.

4. Summarize the following passage to not more than one-third of the original. Give it a suitable title: 10

Passage:

When the study of the learning environment is used as a means of describing learning situations, it improves our understanding of various influences on learning outcomes. In particular, by understanding influences at the level of concrete behaviour, one can more easily determine appropriate interventions for changing the environment. A learning environment comprises "all of the physical surroundings, psychosocial or emotional conditions, and social or cultural influences" present in a learning situation (Hiemstra, 1991, p. 8).

Both the physical and the social aspects of a learning environment influence student participation and satisfaction (Fulton, 1991) and are believed to affect the learning of the people who function in them. These effects can be positive or negative (Vahala & Winston, 1994). In fact, learning environments have effects beyond learning to include socialization, particularly when certain patterns of interaction occur across many classes in a curricular program. Student and faculty come to expect and to see as normative some actions and not others (i.e., what one should or should not do). For example, when students' seats are bolted to the floor facing a lectern, student collaboration can be inhibited. If, in combination with this physical influence, instruction is almost entirely lecture-based, students can come to resist different teaching methods such as student-led discussion or small group work (e.g., Waite, Jackson, & Diwan, 2002).

While the learning environment exists in social space, it is rarely explicitly stated nor are its features static. Instead, the learning environment is negotiated through student-student and instructor-student interaction, and its characteristics, in turn, have a socializing effect (Rorty, 1999). Communication patterns are key, since it is by creating shared understanding that teaching and learning occur. Communication patterns that become typical provide not just information, but represent and maintain social order, implying and prescribing the way things are done or should be done — and who can do them — "around here" (Burke, 1966; Goffman, 1959; Mead, 1934).

BDP / BCA / BTS

Chapter 7: Term-End Examination, December- 2017

FEG-2 : FOUNDATION COURSE IN ENGLISH-2

Time: 2 hours

Maximum Marks: 50

Note: Answer all questions.

1. Write a composition in about 350 words on any one of the following: 20

(a) The importance of kindness and respect in the modern world

(b) Print versus e-books — which one will stay?

(c) Living in harmony with nature

(d) The importance of educating girls

2. Write a paragraph in about 200 words on any one of the following: 10

(a) The season you enjoy the most

(b) Listening to music

(c) The ideal teacher

(d) The role of friends in our lives

3. Write a letter on one of the following: 10

(a) Write a letter to the municipal authorities in your city describing the problems being faced by the residents of your colony as roads have been dug up for sewer lines and then left unrepaired.

OR

(b) Write a letter to the head of your institution pointing out how the campus has been defaced during students' elections. Please give solutions.

4. Read the following passage and make notes in an appropriate format. Give it a suitable title: 10

Passage:

Elderly care, or simply eldercare (also known in parts of the English-speaking world as aged care), is the fulfilment of the special needs and requirements that are unique to senior citizens. This broad term encompasses such services as assisted living, adult day care, long-term care, nursing homes (often referred to as residential care), hospice care, and home care. Because of the wide variety of elderly care found nationally, as well as differentiating cultural perspectives on elderly citizens, it cannot be limited to any one practice. For example, many countries in Asia use government-established elderly care quite infrequently, preferring the traditional methods of being cared for by younger generations of family members.

Elderly care emphasizes the social and personal requirements of senior citizens who need some assistance with daily activities and health care, but who desire to age with dignity. It is an important distinction, in that the design of housing, services, activities, employee training, and such should be truly customer-centred. It is also noteworthy that a large amount of global elderly care falls under the unpaid market sector. The form of elderly care provided varies greatly among countries and is changing rapidly. Even within the same country, regional differences exist with respect to care for the elderly. However, it has been observed that the global elderly consume the most health expenditure out of any other age group. One must also account for an increasingly large proportion of global elderly, especially in developing nations, as continued pressure is put on limiting fertility and decreasing family size.

Traditionally, elderly care has been the responsibility of family members and was provided within the extended family home. Increasingly in modern societies, elderly care is now being provided by the state or charitable institutions. The reasons for this change include decreasing family size, the greater life expectancy of elderly people, the geographical dispersion of families, and the tendency for women to be educated and work outside the home. Although these changes have affected European and North American countries first, they are now increasingly affecting Asian countries as well.

In most western countries, elderly care facilities are residential family care homes, free-standing assisted living facilities, nursing homes, and Continuing Care Retirement Communities (CCRCs). A family care home is a residential home with support and supervisory personnel by an agency, organization, or individual that provides room and board, personal care, and habilitation services in a family environment for at least two and no more than six persons.

BDP / BCA / BTS

Chapter 8: Term-End Examination, June- 2018

FEG-2 : FOUNDATION COURSE IN ENGLISH-2

Time: 2 hours

Maximum Marks: 50

Note: Answer all questions.

1. Write a composition in about 350 words on any one of the following: 20

(a) Friends or Family — who do we rely on most and why?

(b) The interference of social media in personal lives

(c) Television Reality Shows — how real are they?

(d) Keeping our rivers clean

2. Write a paragraph in about 200 words on any one of the following: 10

(a) What do our elders really need?

(b) The importance of having a hobby

(c) Why should we be honest?

(d) Good neighbours

3. Write a letter on one of the following: 10

(a) Write a letter to the President of your Residents Welfare Association pointing out the presence of dangerous street dogs in your area. Suggest solutions.

OR

(b) Write a letter to the Editor of a local newspaper outlining the sorry condition of the neighbourhood parks. Suggest what can be done to revive these 'green lungs' of the city.

4. Read the following passage and make notes in an appropriate format. Give it a suitable title: 10

Passage:

The word success itself is elusive. Everyone has their own definition of what success is, making it very difficult to define how to obtain it. And while you'll have to figure out the details regarding what it takes to be successful in your own personal life or career, the truth is that you can fundamentally change your life for the better by focusing on certain concepts.

Success isn't something you can obtain on your own. While you ultimately define your own path, you're greatly influenced and aided by the people around you. Until you realize this and start to reach out, you'll find it's nearly impossible to break through. Ask yourself this question: Are the people closest to you pushing you in the right direction or holding you back? They're either doing one or the other, so make sure you surround yourself with positive, successful people.

Did you know that Lyndon B. Johnson actually turned down a lucrative oil investment early in his career because he knew that being associated with oil companies could hurt his chances of becoming President one day? Talk about having an incredible amount of foresight. While you may not ever have to make such difficult decisions, you will be challenged on a daily basis. Always keep your priorities in focus and never waver for temporary satisfaction.

When you make a mistake or fail, do you walk away and pursue something else? That's the natural response for most of us. However, you must be willing to embrace failures and recognize them as catalysts for future success.

You'll often hear people talk about a future goal as some far-off thing that will one day manifest. Here's the truth, though: The average life span is only 78 years. This means you only have a few decades to make your mark. It's time to set goals with finite deadlines. This is what successful people do. Do you want to own a business? Set a goal of owning your own business in five years. Do you want to travel the world? Set a goal of visiting a new country every summer. Successful goals always have timelines.

Do what makes you happy and you'll soon create your own definition of success. You should be wary of anyone who defines success. The reality is that there's no concrete explanation. With that being said, there are a variety of things you can do to discover success in your life. Keep in mind that what works for you will be quite different than what works for the next person in line.

BDP / BCA / BTS

Chapter 9: Term-End Examination, December- 2018

FEG-2 : FOUNDATION COURSE IN ENGLISH-2

Time: 2 hours

Maximum Marks: 50

Note: Answer all questions.

1. Write a composition in about 350 words on any one of the following: 20

(a) Global warming and its effect on our environment

(b) The challenges that I have overcome in life

(c) The true religion is the religion of humanity

(d) Breakdown in personal relationships in the modern world

2. Write a paragraph in about 200 words on any one of the following: 10

(a) My favourite place at home

(b) Ways to remain healthy

(c) Hostel life vs. life at home with parents

(d) Alternate sources of energy

3. Answer one of the following: 10

(a) You are part of a 'Nature Watch' group which is working towards making your city/neighbourhood 'plastic bag-free'. A meeting of your group was organized which was attended by the Executive Body members, Block level leaders and volunteers. Among the points discussed were:

(i) The enormity of the problem

(ii) The plan of action

(iii) Places/Persons to target

(iv) Difficulties envisaged

(v) Overcoming the difficulties, etc.

Write a report for the local daily taking care to include all the significant details.

OR

(b) Provide your ideas on the statement:

"Speak only when your words are more beautiful than the silence."

Your writing should explain, analyse, compare and illustrate the statement given above.

4. Summarize the following passage to not more than one-third of the original. Give it a suitable title: 10

Passage:

Do you have the right to have an opinion? When do you have the right to have an opinion? Who has the right to have an opinion?

At one extreme we can have a person who knows very little about a subject and yet comes out with a strong opinion on that subject. At the other extreme is someone who is well-informed and has thought a lot about the subject, but is unable to express an opinion.

An opinion is a sort of stew of information, perception, feelings and values cooked together within a particular culture.

Why have opinions? You might as well ask, 'Why have people?' It is possible to imagine a discussion in which no one has an opinion. There is a mutual exploration of the subject. At some point, however, values need to get attached and that attachment results in an opinion.

There may be opinions which are very strongly held. There may be tentative opinions which are a sort of 'holding position' until a better opinion forms. There may be opinions which are held quite firmly but still open to change.

You can contemplate an extensive menu in a restaurant but at some stage you have to order a particular dish — even if you are torn between two.

A beautiful mind is capable of forming opinions and is not afraid to do so. At the same time, the beautiful mind is always conscious of the basis for that opinion. Furthermore, any opinion held is open to change. This is not unlike a scientific hypothesis. The hypothesis is definite and usable otherwise no experiments could ever be designed. Yet the hypothesis is only 'provisional' and the scientist is always seeking to form a better one.

BDP / BCA / BTS

Chapter 10: Term-End Examination, June 2019

FEG-2 : FOUNDATION COURSE IN ENGLISH-2

Time: 2 hours **Maximum Marks: 50**

Note: Answer all questions.

1. Write a composition in about 350 words on any one of the following: 20

(a) The importance of obeying traffic rules

(b) Why do we take photographs?

(c) TV as a medium of education

(d) Boy

2. Write a paragraph in about 200 words on any one of the following: 10

(a) Understanding the mind of teenagers

(b) Why should we be courteous to people?

(c) Are books going out of our lives?

(d) Real friends and virtual friends

3. Answer one of the following: 10

(a) Write a letter to the Municipal Councillor of your area pointing out that roads have been dug up and left unrepaired for months. Outline the problems that have resulted and seek speedy action.

OR

(b) Write a letter to the editor of a local newspaper regarding indiscriminate felling of trees to construct buildings in the city. Describe what effects it will have and offer solutions.

4. Read the following passage and make notes in a suitable format. Give it a suitable title. 10

Music is an art form and cultural activity whose medium is sound organized in time. The common elements of music are pitch, rhythm, dynamics and the sonic qualities of timbre and texture. Music is performed with a vast range of instruments and vocal techniques ranging from singing to rapping; there are solely instrumental pieces, solely vocal pieces and pieces that combine singing and instruments.

In its most general form, the activities describing music as an art form or cultural activity include the creation of works of music, the criticism of music, the study of the history of music, and the aesthetic examination of music. Ancient Greek and Indian philosophers defined music as tones ordered horizontally as melodies and vertically as harmonies. Common sayings such as "the harmony of the spheres" and "it is music to my ears" point to the notion that music is often ordered and pleasant to listen to. The creation, performance, significance, and even the definition of music vary according to culture and social context. There are many types of music, including popular music, traditional music, art music, music written for religious ceremonies and work songs such as chanteys. Music ranges from strictly organized compositions such as classical music symphonies from the 1700s and 1800s, through to spontaneously played improvisational music such as jazz, and avant-garde styles of chance-based contemporary music from the 20th and 21st centuries. Music can be divided into genres and genres can be further divided into subgenres although the dividing lines and relationships between music genres are often subtle, sometimes open to personal interpretation, and occasionally controversial. Within the arts, music may be classified as a performing art, a fine art or as an auditory art. Music may be played or sung and heard live at a rock concert or orchestra performance, heard live as part of a dramatic work or it may be recorded and listened to on a radio, MP3 player, CD player, smartphone or as film score or TV show.

In many cultures, music is an important part of people's way of life, as it plays a key role in religious rituals, rite of passage ceremonies, social and cultural activities ranging from amateur karaoke singing to playing in an amateur funk band or singing in a community choir. People may make music as a hobby or work as a professional musician or singer. The music industry includes the individuals who create new songs and musical pieces;individuals who perform music, individuals who record music, individuals who organize concert tours, and individuals who sell recordings and sheet music and scores to customers.

BDP / BCA / BTS

Chapter 11:Term-End Examination, December- 2019

FEG-2 : FOUNDATION COURSE IN ENGLISH-2

Time: 2 Hours

Maximum Marks: 50

Note: Answer all questions.

1. Write a composition in about 350 words on any one of the following: 20

(a) Childhood Memories

(b) The role of music in our lives

(c) Why should we love hobbies?

(d) Should celebrities endorse all kinds of products?

2. Write a paragraph in about 200 words on any one of the following: 10

(a) Our teachers in primary school

(b) The influence of films on our lives

(c) The importance of taking a break from daily routine

(d) Why should we travel?

3. Answer one of the following: 10

(a) Write a letter to the Head of Traffic Police in your city describing the frequent jams in your area. Outline the difficulties and offer solutions.

OR

(b) Write a letter to the Principal of your institution regarding the bad condition of your hostel and mess food. State inconveniences and suggest improvements.

4. Read the following passage and make notes in a suitable format. Give it a suitable title:

10

Passage:

Norway is a unitary sovereign state whose territory comprises the western portion of the Scandinavian Peninsula plus the remote island of Jan Mayen and the archipelago of Svalbard. Norway has a total area of 385,252 square kilometres and a population of 5,258,317. The country shares a long eastern border with Sweden and is bordered by Finland and Russia to the north-east, and the Skagerrak strait to the south, with Denmark on the other side. Norway has an extensive coastline, facing the North Atlantic Ocean and the Barents Sea.

King Harald V of the Dano-German House of Glucksburg is the current King of Norway. Erna Solberg became Prime Minister in 2013 and was reelected in September 2017. A constitutional monarchy, Norway divides state power between the Parliament, the cabinet, and the Supreme Court. The kingdom was established as a merger of a large number of petty kingdoms. By the traditional count from the year 872, the kingdom has existed continuously for 1,145 years, and the list of Norwegian monarchs includes over sixty kings and earls.

Norway has both administrative and political subdivisions on two levels: counties and municipalities. It maintains close ties with both the European Union and the United States. Norway is a founding member of the United Nations, NATO, the European Free Trade Association, the Council of Europe, the Antarctic Treaty, and the Nordic Council; a member of the European Economic Area, the WTO, and the OECD; and a part of the Schengen Area.

Norway offers universal health care and a comprehensive social security system, and Norwegian Society's values are rooted in egalitarian ideals. The Norwegian state owns key industrial sectors such as oil and hydropower with extensive reserves of petroleum, natural gas, minerals, lumber, seafood, and fresh water. The petroleum industry accounts for around a quarter of the country's gross domestic product (GDP). On a per-capita basis, Norway is the world's largest producer of oil and gas outside the Middle East.

The country has the fourth-highest per capita income in the world on the World Bank and IMF lists. It has the world's largest sovereign wealth fund, with a value of USD 1 trillion. Norway has had the highest Human Development Index ranking in the world since 2009, a position also held previously between 2001 and 2006. It also has the highest inequality-adjusted ranking. Norway ranks first on the World Happiness Report, the OECD Better Life Index, the Index of Public Integrity, and the Democracy Index. Norway also has one of the lowest crime rates in the world

BDP-BCA-BTS

Chapter 12: Term-End Examination, June- 2020

FEG-2: FOUNDATION COURSE IN ENGLISH-2

Time: 2 Hours

Maximum Marks: 50

Note: Answer all questions.

1. Write a composition in about 350 words on any one of the following: **20**

(a) A well-groomed personality contributes to success in all walks of life.

(b) Online transaction of money is a boon for curbing corruption.

(c) Advantages of eating healthy and natural foods.

(d) Swachh Bharat or Clean India campaign should begin at home.

2. Write a paragraph in about 200 words on any one of the following: **10**

(a) The activity I enjoy the most

(b) Reading fiction

(c) If I were a teacher!

(d) The role of neighbours in society.

3. Write a letter to the municipal authorities in your city describing the menace of loud speakers being used in marriage venues and banquet halls in and around your residence. Give suggestions to solve the problem. 10

Or

Write a letter to the head of your institution requesting permission to organize a blood donation camp on the campus. 10

4. Read the following passage and make notes in an appropriate format. Give it a suitable title: **10**

Web blogging or blogging as it is more commonly known, is a way of keeping a diary online. One unique feature is that it is in a reverse chronological order, meaning that the newest entry always appears first. Although blogs are sometimes described as diaries, they can be so much more than just an online version of what was traditionally a handwritten record of personal thoughts and ideas. Blogs do present an individual's thoughts, but blogs can also contain video clips, photos, MP3 sound clips, links to news articles and much more.

One way of understanding the difference between a blog and a diary could be in looking at the difference between newspapers and television. While you get a mental picture about the force of a hurricane from a written description in a newspaper, this does not compare to the vivid realism that you get from a television clip showing the hurricane in action. A blogger can simply present so much more information in a very concise way.

Like many technological innovations, blogging can trace its origins back to earlier innovations. Its development came after the development of new types of software and ways of communicating online in the early 1990s. Email lists and bulletin board systems (BBS) allowed people to post messages that a large group of people could read and respond to with their own messages. In short, the new media allowed users to carry on conversations over time and distance. When early bloggers, such as Justin Hall and James alba' Parry began posting, the 'Telogosphere' was a fairly limited space. Many early bloggers created formulas by updating their webpages. It was not until 1997 when developments in blogging software appeared that made blogging more accessible to the general public. Today, blogs are everywhere. In 2005, the Blog Herald estimated the number of blogs to exceed 100 million worldwide.

So what are these blogs about? Blogs are about as varied as the number of people writing them. Blogs can be about anything and, in some cases, nothing at all. Besides the countless individuals digitally detailing their daily existence, many in the media spotlight have turned to this medium to help get their own message out. From celebrities like Madonna to companies like Microsoft, brands are now using them to help communicate with their audience. It has proven a relatively cheap way to handle PR and marketing.

BDP / BCA / BTS

Chapter 13: Term-End Examination, February- 2021

FEG-2: FOUNDATION COURSE IN ENGLISH-2

Time: 2 Hours

Maximum Marks: 50

Note: Answer all questions.

1. Write a composition in about 350 words on any one of the following: **20**

(a) One cannot demand respect but one can command it.

(b) The younger generation must develop reading habits.

(c) Spending more time on social networking leads to waste of precious time.

(d) The teaching profession demands intelligence and aptitude.

2. Write a paragraph in about 200 words on any one of the following: **10**

(a) The festival that I love to celebrate the most

(b) The benefits of walking daily

(c) My ideal friend

(d) The role of teachers in our lives

3. Write a letter to the civic authorities describing the menace of stray dogs in your colony.(10)

Or

Write a letter to the head of your institution requesting permission to organize a half marathon to spread the message of keeping fit. **10**

4. Read the following passage and make notes in an appropriate format. Give it a suitable title: **10**

Teachers and other education professionals spend a lot of time testing, evaluating and assessing students. Sometimes this is to measure the students' abilities to see if they can enter a course or institution. Sometimes it is to see how well they get on. Sometimes it is because the students themselves want a qualification. Sometimes this assessment is formal and public, and sometimes it is informal and takes place in day-to-day lessons.

We can make a difference between summative and formative assessment. Summative assessment, as the name suggests, is the kind of measurement that takes place to round things off or make a one-off measurement. Such tests include the end-of-year tests that students take or the big public exams which many students enter for. Formative assessment, on the other hand, relates to the kind of feedback teachers give students as a course is progressing and which, as a result, may help them to improve their performance. This is done at a micro level every time we indicate that something is wrong and help students to get it right, but can also take place when teachers go through the results of progress and achievement tests. The result of such formative assessments could well, in certain circumstances, suggest that the teacher change the focus of the curriculum or the emphasis he or she is giving to certain lesson elements.

Formative assessment, in other words, means that teachers as well as students may have to change and develop. It is perhaps because of this that many teachers are not keen on adopting a rigorous approach to formative testing, quite apart from the fact that in many institutions such ongoing modification is not encouraged. However, it is worth remembering that handing back any piece of assessed homework or progress test presents teachers and students with ideal learning opportunities — opportunities which will be wasted if the work is immediately put away, rather than being used as a vehicle for development.

There are various reasons for testing. One of the reasons is the placement test which facilitates placing students in the right class at the right level. Usually based on syllabuses and materials the students will follow and use once their level has been decided on, these test grammar and vocabulary knowledge and assess students' productive and receptive skills. Some schools ask students to assess themselves as part of the placement process, adding this self-analysis into final placing decision.

BDP/BCA/BTS

Chapter 14: Term-End Examination, June- 2021

FEG-2: FOUNDATION COURSE IN ENGLISH–2

Time: 2 Hours

Maximum Marks: 50

Note: Answer all questions.

1. Write a composition in about 350 words on any one of the following: **20**

(a) The importance of kindness.
(b) My experiences as a school student.
(c) The break up of the Indian joint family.
(d) The drawbacks of technology.

2. Write a paragraph of about 200 words on any one of the following: **10**

(a) Virtual friends

(b) A trip made with family

(c) My mother

(d) I wish I could be ....

3. You are a member of your residents' welfare association and recently attended a meeting held to discuss the increasing number of thefts in your area. The meeting was attended by all the office bearers, some residents, and members of the local police. Points of discussion were:

(a) Necessity of appointing night watchman

(b) Increasing the number of street lights

(c) Regular police patrolling

(d) Forming a volunteer residents patrol

(e) Difficulties

(f) Solutions

Write a report to be submitted to the local administration and the police including all important details. 10

Or

Give your views on the following statement: "A strong person speaks in a quiet voice." Explain and analyze with examples. 10

4. Summarize the following passage in not more than one-third of the original. Give it a suitable title: **10**

Road safety is a crucial issue, and it is the duty of parents to educate their children about how they must follow traffic rules and signs while negotiating traffic on the road. In major metro cities of India, every year, an entire week is dedicated to the observation of road safety measures. The Transport departments of different states bring out catchy slogans, put up posters and distribute leaflets in schools and colleges to create awareness regarding road safety. Many of us have a habit of running across a road and disregarding traffic signals that often result in horrific accidents. By knowing and practicing pedestrian rules, we can at least make sure of remaining unhurt.

When young, children generally imbibe everything that they see. Consequently, if they are taught how they should behave or walk on the road at an early age, they develop awareness and behave in a way that helps them to avoid accidents. After all, they are the future of the world. We must know the significance of zebra crossings and should make a habit of using them while crossing the road, which is not seen very often on Indian roads, unfortunately. It is not only when walking but while driving too that we must strictly follow certain rules like wearing seat belts, maintaining a safe distance from another vehicle and not overspeeding so as to ensure that no accidents occur on the road.

There are three types of road safety signs — mandatory, cautionary and informatory that enlighten us about the condition of the road ahead and instruct us regarding what we need to do at relevant junctions and crossroads. By paying attention to these signs and remaining alert at all times, we can ensure that we do not run into problems.

A death constitutes the greatest irreparable loss and generates a void that can never be filled. And when it happens due to a moment of carelessness on the street, there is no assuaging the grief. Hence, conscious efforts should be taken by everyone so that each one of us, when we are out of our homes may return safely.

BDP/BCA/BTS

Chapter 15: Term-End Examination, December- 2021

FEG-2: FOUNDATION COURSE IN ENGLISH–2

Time: 2 Hours

Maximum Marks: 50

Note: Answer all questions.

1. Write a composition in about 350 words on any one of the following: **20**

(a) The importance of following traffic rules

(b) What I admire most about my parents

(c) Our responsibilities towards the elderly

(d) The role of hobbies in shaping a child's personality

2. Write a paragraph of about 200 words on any one of the following: **10**

(a) My way of overcoming stress

(b) Why we should respect women

(c) Public transport or private vehicles

(d) How I wish ....

3. You are a member of an amateur football club. You attended a meeting with leading sportsmen, officials, and funding organizations to discuss:

(a) Lack of playing fields

(b) Insufficient support from schools and families

(c) Not enough coaches and sports kits

(d) Difficulty in generating funds

(e) Possible solutions

Write a report based on the discussion for your local newspaper. 10

Or

Give your views on the following statement: "One picture is worth a thousand words." Explain, analyze, and offer examples. 10

4. Summarize the following passage in not more than one-third of the original. Give it a suitable title: **10**

Reading is probably one of the most beneficial and feasible activities that anyone can do. It is through reading that a person discovers new ideas, concepts, places, and people. Some people even describe reading as a journey that starts as the opening of a page, and finishes as the last page is turned. The reason why reading is so important is because reading is relaxing to our mind and soul; it is a way for children to reach out to the world, and it improves our thinking process. There is something about stopping to focus on words during reading that is instantly relaxing. Maybe it is just staying still in a chair, something that does not seem to happen often in our lives. Stress is a major concern for a lot of people because of the day-to-day labor. Even if we have a stressful day, a book can easily distract us from our own problems. Reading has the ability to calm us down and dispense peace. Reading should be encouraged among children at an early age. It is no secret that reading increases children's vocabulary and improves spelling more than talking or direct teaching. Reading forces us to look at words that we might not have seen or heard in our lives. In fact, language in children's books is likely to be more complicated than their average conversation. A large number of children who read are articulate while the others are not. Reading improves our thinking process as it requires readers to imagine and think about characters and plot. It also obliges readers to focus on what they are reading for long periods. Unlike magazines, internet posts, or e-mails that might contain small pieces of information, books tell the whole story.

Since the readers must concentrate in order to read, they will improve their concentration and thinking ability. If we want to be known as persons of depth and intelligence, we must start cultivating the habit of reading regularly. "No entertainment is so cheap as reading, or any pleasure so lasting." (Montagu). Reading is our companion that assists us to go through life by not only refreshing us but by giving us a great outlook towards life.

BDP/BCA/BTS

Chapter 16: Term-End Examination, June- 2022

FEG-2: FOUNDATION COURSE IN ENGLISH-2

Time: 2 Hours

Maximum Marks: 50

Note: Answer all questions.

1. Write a composition in about 350 words on any one of the following: **20**

(a) The role of friends in our lives

(b) The importance of reading

(c) Sports and health

(d) Environmental pollution

2. Write a paragraph in about 200 words on any one of the following: **10**

(a) Holidays

(b) Parents

(c) Discipline is the road to success

(d) Why should we follow traffic rules?

3. Write a letter to the editor of your local newspaper regarding the accumulation of garbage in your residential area. Outline the problems and offer solutions. 10

OR

Write a letter to the President of your students' union, describing the sorry state of the campus after students' union elections. Mention why it is a matter of concern and offer constructive suggestions. 10

4. Read the following passage and make notes in an appropriate format. Give it a suitable title: **10**

Space exploration is the use of astronomy and space technology to explore outer space. While the study of space is carried out mainly by astronomers with telescopes, its physical exploration though is conducted both by unmanned robotic space probes and human spaceflight. While the observation of objects in space, known as astronomy, predates reliable recorded history, it was the development of large and relatively efficient rockets during the mid-twentieth century that allowed physical space exploration to become a reality. Common rationales for exploring space include advancing scientific research, national prestige, uniting different nations, ensuring the future survival of humanity, and developing military and strategic advantages against other countries.

Space exploration has often been used as a proxy competition for geopolitical rivalries such as the Cold War. The early era of space exploration was driven by a 'Space Race' between the Soviet Union and the United States. The launch of the first human-made object to orbit Earth, the Soviet Union's Sputnik 1, on 4th October, 1957, and the first Moon landing by the American Apollo 11 mission on 20th July, 1969 are often taken as landmarks for this initial period. The Soviet space programme achieved many of the first milestones, including the first living being in orbit in 1957, the first human spaceflight (Yuri Gagarin aboard Vostok 1) in 1961, the first spacewalk (by Alexei Leonov) on 18th March, 1965, the first automatic landing on another celestial body in 1966, and the launch of the first space station (Salyut 1) in 1971. After the first 20 years of exploration, focus shifted from one-off flights to renewable hardware, such as the Space Shuttle programme, and from competition to cooperation as with the International Space Station (ISS).

The first telescope was said to be invented in 1608 in the Netherlands by an eyeglass-maker named Hans Lippershey. The Orbiting Astronomical Observatory 2 was the first space telescope launched on 7th December, 1968. As of 2nd February, 2019, there were 3,891 confirmed exoplanets discovered. The Milky Way is estimated to contain 100 – 400 billion stars and more than 100 billion planets. There are at least 2 trillion galaxies in the observable universe. GN-z11 is the most distant known object from the Earth, reported as 32 billion light-years away.

BDP/BCA/BTS

Chapter 17: Term-End Examination, December- 2022

FEG-2: FOUNDATION COURSE IN ENGLISH-2

Time: 2 Hours

Maximum Marks: 50

Note: Answer all questions.

1. Write a composition in about 350 words on any one of the following: 20

(a) The Importance of Physical Fitness

(b) Why do we need Public Libraries?

(c) Advantages of Social Media

(d) The Impact of Cinema on Youngsters

2. Write a paragraph in about 200 words on any one of the following: 10

(a) Time Management

(b) Student Life

(c) Respect for Women

(d) Good Manners

3. Write a letter to the Municipal Councillor of your area regarding the increasing number of stray dogs in your locality. Outline the dangers and offer constructive solutions. 10

Or

Write a letter to the warden of your college hostel describing the unhygienic state of the hostel's washrooms and kitchen sinks. State why it is a matter of concern and offer suggestions for improvement. 10

4. Read the following passage and make notes in an appropriate format. Give it a suitable title: 10

Air pollution comes from both natural and human-made (anthropogenic) sources. However, globally human-made pollutants from combustion, construction, mining, agriculture and warfare

are increasingly significant in the air pollution equation. Motor vehicle emissions are one of the leading causes of air pollution. Principal stationary pollution sources include chemical plants, coal-fired power plants, oil refineries, petrochemical plants, nuclear waste disposal activity, incinerators, large livestock farms (dairy cows, pigs, poultry, etc.), PVC factories, metals production factories, plastics factories, and other heavy industry. Agricultural air pollution comes from contemporary practices which include clear felling and burning of natural vegetation as well as spraying of pesticides and herbicides.

About 400 million metric tons of hazardous wastes are generated each year. In February 2007, a report by the Intergovernmental Panel on Climate Change (IPCC), representing the work of 2,500 scientists, economists, and policy-makers from more than 120 countries, said that humans have been the primary cause of global warming since 1950. Humans have ways to cut greenhouse gas emissions and avoid the consequences of global warming, a major climate report concluded. But to change the climate, the transition from fossil fuels like coal and oil needs to occur within decades, according to the final report this year from the UN's Intergovernmental Panel on Climate Change (IPCC).

Some of the more common soil contaminants are chlorinated hydrocarbons (CFH), heavy metals (such as chromium, cadmium — found in rechargeable batteries, and lead — found in lead paint, aviation fuel and still in some countries, gasoline), MTBE, zinc, arsenic and benzene. Ordinary municipal landfills are the source of many chemical substances entering the soil environment (and often groundwater), emanating from the wide variety of refuse accepted, especially substances illegally discarded there, or from pre-1970 landfills that may have been subject to little control in the US or EU. There have also been some unusual releases of polychlorinated dibenzodioxins, commonly called dioxins for simplicity, such as TCDD.

Pollution can also be the consequence of a natural disaster. For example, hurricanes often involve water contamination from sewage, and petrochemical spills from ruptured boats or automobiles. Larger scale and environmental damage is not uncommon when coastal oil rigs or refineries are involved. Some sources of pollution, such as nuclear power plants or oil tankers, can produce widespread and potentially hazardous releases when accidents occur.

BDP/BCA/BTS

Chapter 18: Term-End Examination, June- 2023

FEG-2: FOUNDATION COURSE IN ENGLISH–II

Time: 2 Hours

Maximum Marks: 50

Note: Answer all questions.

1. Write a composition in about 350 words on any one of the following: 20

(a) Politeness is the hallmark of an educated person.

(b) Caring for the elderly.

(c) The importance of hobbies.

(d) Power should be kind.

2. Write a paragraph of about 200 words on any one of the following: 10

(a) What I like about my family.

(b) Enjoying leisure time.

(c) The importance of daily exercise.

(d) The writer whose books I enjoy reading.

3. Write a letter to the Secretary of your Residents Welfare Association regarding the general upkeep of the area. List the problems and offer solutions. 10

Or

Write a letter to the head of your institution requesting permission to felicitate eminent sportswomen. 10

4. Read the following passage and make notes in an appropriate format. Give it a suitable title: 10

A good business letter is one that gets results. The best way to get results is to develop a letter that, in its appearance, style and content, conveys information efficiently. To perform this function, a business letter should be concise, clear and courteous.

The business letter must be concise: don't waste words. Little introduction or preliminary chat is necessary. Get to the point, make the point, and leave it. It is safe to assume that your letter is being read by a very busy person with all kinds of papers to deal with. Re-read and revise your message until the words and sentences you have used are precise. This takes time, but is a necessary part of a good business letter. A short business letter that makes its point quickly has much more impact on a reader than a long-winded, rambling exercise in creative writing. This does not mean that there is no place for style and even, on occasion, humour in the business letter. While it conveys a message in its contents, the letter also provides the reader with an impression of you, its author: the medium is part of the message.

The business letter must be clear. You should have a very firm idea of what you want to say, and you should let the reader know it. Use the structure of the letter—the paragraphs, topic sentences, introduction and conclusion—to guide the reader point by point from your thesis, through your reasoning, to your conclusion. Paragraph often, to break up the page and to lend an air of organisation to the letter. Use an accepted business-letter format. Re-read what you have written from the point of view of someone who is seeing it for the first time, and be sure that all explanations are adequate, all information provided (including reference numbers, dates, and other identification). A clear message, clearly delivered, is the essence of business communication.

The business letter must be courteous. Sarcasm and insults are ineffective and can often work against you. If you are sure you are right, point that out as politely as possible, explain why you are right, and outline what the reader is expected to do about it. Another form of courtesy is taking care in your writing and typing of the business letter. Grammatical and spelling errors (even if you call them typing errors) tell a reader that you don't think enough of him or can lower the reader's opinion of your personality faster than anything you say, no matter how idiotic. There are excuses for ignorance;

there are no excuses for sloppiness. The business letter is your custom-made representative. It speaks for you and is a permanent record of your message. It can pay big dividends on the time you invest in giving it a concise message, a clear structure, and a courteous tone.

9 789369 723249

Printed at Repro India Ltd.